ENVIRONMENT
Infographics

Chris Oxlade

Raintree is an imprint of Capstone Global Library Limited,
a company incorporated in England and Wales having its
registered office at 7 Pilgrim Street, London, EC4V 6LB –
Registered company number: 6695582

www.raintreepublishers.co.uk
myorders@raintreepublishers.co.uk

Text © Capstone Global Library Limited 2014
First published in hardback in 2014
The moral rights of the proprietor have been asserted.

Edited by Rebecca Rissman, Dan Nunn, and
   John-Paul Wilkins
Designed by Philippa Jenkins
Original illustrations © Capstone Global Library Ltd 2014
Illustrations by HL Studios
Picture research by Elizabeth Alexander
Production by Vicki Fitzgerald
Originated by Capstone Global Library Ltd
Printed and bound in China

ISBN 978 1 406 272210 9
17 16 15 14 13
10 9 8 7 6 5 4 3 2 1

British Library Cataloguing in Publication Data
Oxlade, Chris.
Environment. – (Infographics)
A full catalogue record for this book is available from the
British Library.

Acknowledgements
We would like to thank the following for permission to
reproduce photographs: Capstone Global Library p. 4;
Shutterstock pp. 4 (© M.Stasy, © Pakhnyushcha, © Stella
Caraman, © Thomas Bethge), 28 (© Complot).

We would like to thank Diana Bentley and Marla Conn for
their invaluable help in the preparation of this book.

Every effort has been made to contact copyright holders of
any material reproduced in this book. Any omissions will
be rectified in subsequent printings if notice is given to the
publisher.

Disclaimer
All the internet addresses (URLs) given in this book were valid
at the time of going to press. However, due to the dynamic
nature of the internet, some addresses may have changed, or
sites may have changed or ceased to exist since publication.
While the author and publisher regret any inconvenience this
may cause readers, no responsibility for any such changes
can be accepted by either the author or the publisher.

CONTENTS

Some words are shown in bold,
like this. You can find out what they
mean by looking in the glossary.

ABOUT INFOGRAPHICS

An infographic is a picture that gives you information. Infographics can be graphs, charts, maps, or other sorts of pictures. The infographics in this book are about the environment.

Infographics make information easier to understand. We see infographics all over the place, every day. They appear in books, newspapers, on the television, on websites, on posters, and in adverts.

How much water we use

Here is a simple infographic.
It shows how much water one
family uses each day.

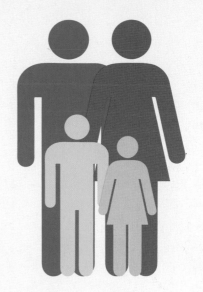

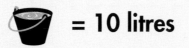 = 10 litres

Average UK household

WATER

What do we use water for?

This infographic shows how we use water for different things.

This number is a percentage. 27% means 27 litres out of every 100 litres.

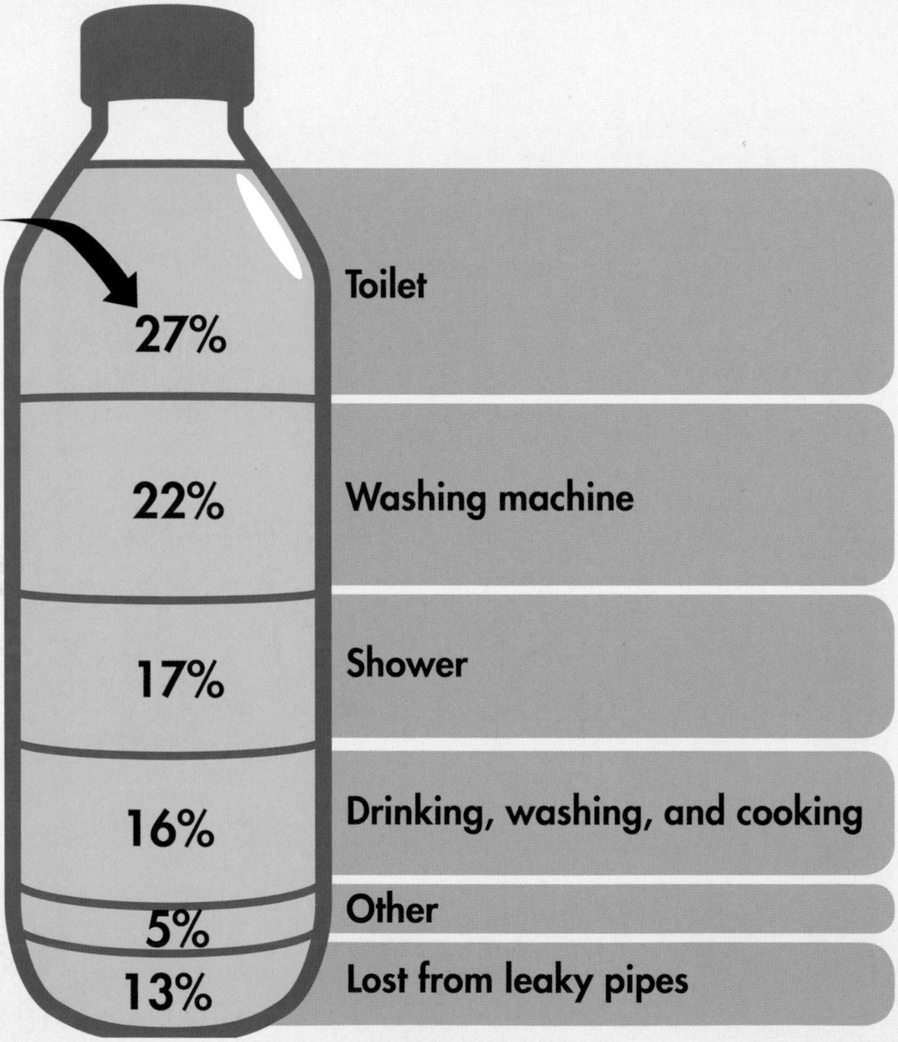

27% Toilet

22% Washing machine

17% Shower

16% Drinking, washing, and cooking

5% Other

13% Lost from leaky pipes

How much water?

This infographic shows how much water different activities use up at home.

 flushing the toilet
11 litres

 having a shower
8 litres a minute

 washing machine
100 litres

 running a tap
4 litres a minute

 filling a bath
8 litres a minute

 dishwasher load
40 litres

Farms and factories need much more water than homes. This graph shows how much water is used in farming and industry, compared with at home.

10%
Homes

20%
Industry

70%
Farming

Water use around the world?

People in different countries use different amounts of water. Some use lots, some use only a little. This map shows how much water a person uses every day in different places.

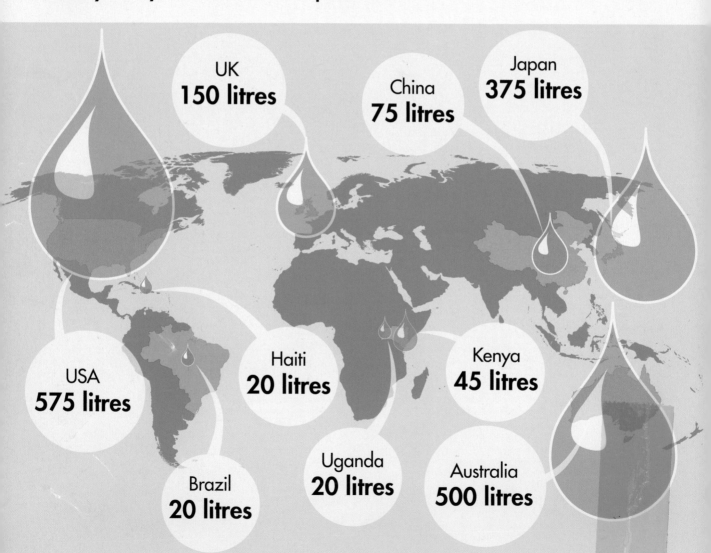

UK
150 litres

China
75 litres

Japan
375 litres

USA
575 litres

Haiti
20 litres

Kenya
45 litres

Brazil
20 litres

Uganda
20 litres

Australia
500 litres

Saving water

Water is precious. In some parts of the world there is not enough to go round. Using less water is also good for the environment. This chart shows some ways to save water, and how much water they save.

 Put a plastic bottle of water in the toilet cistern **1 litre** per flush

 Have a shower instead of a bath Up to **40 litres**

 Mend a leaky tap Up to **20 litres** a day

 Turn off the tap when you brush your teeth **8** litres

 Sponge the car instead of hosing Up to **150 litres**

Bath vs shower

This chart shows how much water you use by taking a shower instead of taking a bath.

Water used to have a five-minute shower **40 litres**

Water used to have a bath **80 litres**

WASTE

Every day we throw away waste, such as food packets and empty tin cans. This infographic shows how much waste people in the United Kingdom make.

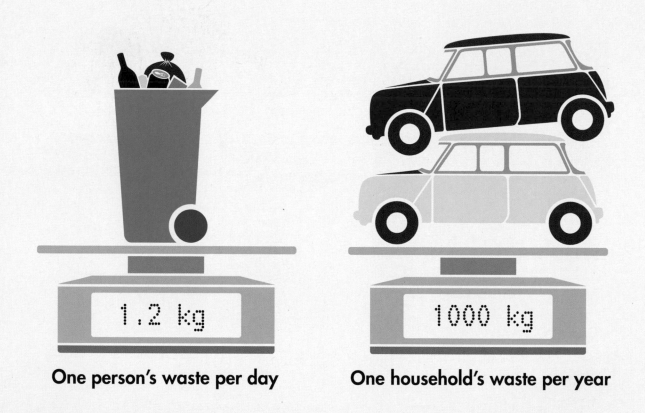

One person's waste per day

One household's waste per year

What sort of waste?

This pie chart shows how much of each sort of waste people in the United States throw away each year.

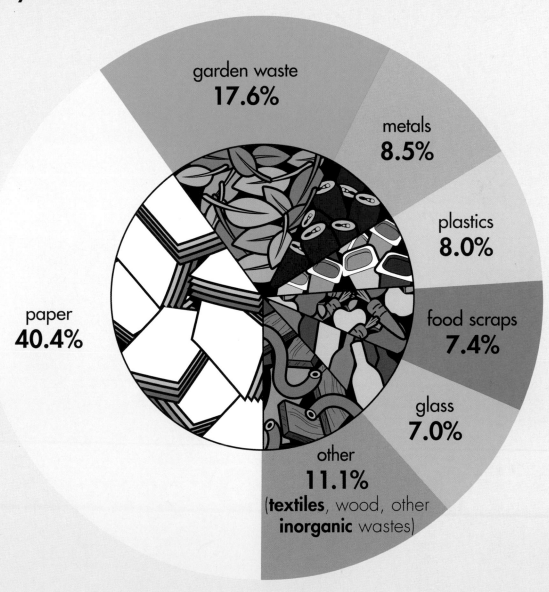

garden waste
17.6%

metals
8.5%

plastics
8.0%

paper
40.4%

food scraps
7.4%

glass
7.0%

other
11.1%
(**textiles**, wood, other **inorganic** wastes)

Waste in the ground

In many countries, most waste is buried in the ground. This is called **landfill**. This infographic shows how much of the United States' waste goes into landfill, and how much is burned or **recycled**.

14%
burned

31%
recycled

55%
landfill

Rotting away

Waste that we put in the ground slowly rots away. This infographic shows how long different sorts of waste take to rot away.

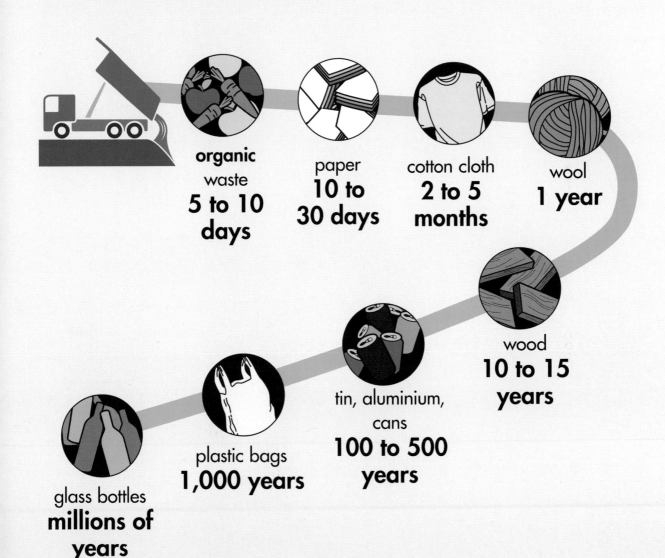

organic waste
5 to 10 days

paper
10 to 30 days

cotton cloth
2 to 5 months

wool
1 year

wood
10 to 15 years

tin, aluminium, cans
100 to 500 years

plastic bags
1,000 years

glass bottles
millions of years

RECYCLING

Plastic bottle recycling facts

This infographic shows some facts about **recycling** plastic bottles.

1 in 4
The number of plastic bottles that are recycled in the UK

36 billion
The number of plastic water bottles sold in the US each year

20
The number of large plastic bottles needed to make a recycled rucksack

15 million
The number of plastic bottles thrown away in the UK every day

6 hours
The length of time a 60 watt light bulb could be powered by using the energy saved from recycling one plastic bottle instead of making a new one

Aluminium recycling facts

Here are some facts about recycling aluminium drinks cans.

6,000
New aluminium drinks cans made in the United States every second

60 days
The time between throwing an aluminium can away and its aluminium getting back on the shelves of a shop in another can

3 hours
The length of time a television can be powered by using the energy saved from recycling one aluminium drinks can instead of making a new one

56 billion
The number of aluminium cans recycled in the United States every year

Paper recycling facts

Here are some facts about recycling paper.

24
The number of trees that have to be cut down to make 1 tonne of newspapers

12.5 million tonnes
The total weight of paper and card used in the UK each year

38 kilograms
The average weight of newspapers bought by each person in the UK each year

29,000 litres
The amount of water saved by recycling a tonne of paper

15

What do we recycle?

This chart shows the amount of different materials that are **recycled** in the UK each year.

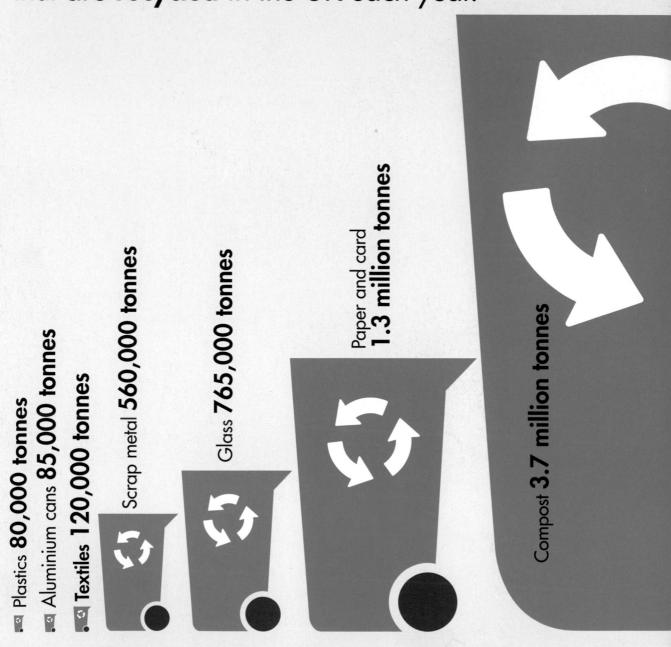

Plastics **80,000 tonnes**

Aluminium cans **85,000 tonnes**

Textiles **120,000 tonnes**

Scrap metal **560,000 tonnes**

Glass **765,000 tonnes**

Paper and card **1.3 million tonnes**

Compost **3.7 million tonnes**

The best recyclers

This map shows how much waste different countries recycle.

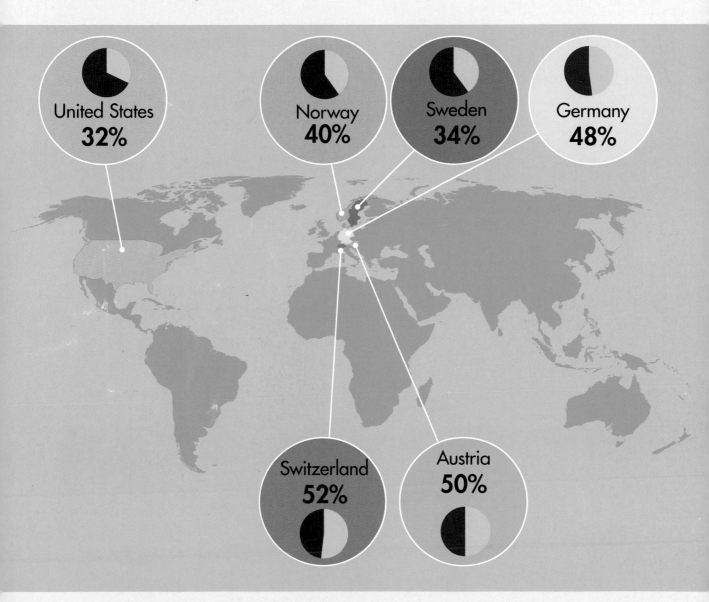

United States
32%

Norway
40%

Sweden
34%

Germany
48%

Switzerland
52%

Austria
50%

POLLUTION

Pollution is waste that goes into rivers, lakes, and the sea, into the air, and onto the land. Pollution is bad for the environment because it harms plants and animals and the places where they live.

Plastic bags are one of the worst sorts of pollution. Here are some facts about plastic-bag pollution.

1.2 trillion
The number of plastic bags used every year in the world

1 million
The number of seabirds killed each year by eating plastic bags and other plastics

12 minutes
The average time that a plastic bag is used for

6 in 100
The number of plastic bags that are **recycled** in Europe

1,200
The number of plastic bags used by each person in the United States every year

1,000 years
The **estimated** time it takes for a plastic bag to rot away

Rubbish on the beach

Lots of waste is washed up on beaches. This infographic shows how many bits of different waste were found on beaches in San Diego County in the United States in one year.

55,100
cigarettes and butts

5,800
plastic lids, cups
and straws

10,150
bits of paper

4,350
bits of glass

5,800
plastic bottle caps

14,500
bits of **styrofoam**

2,900
plastic bags

10,150
plastic food wrappers

15,950
other plastic things

20,300
other things

The biggest oil spills

Oil is pumped from under the sea by oil rigs, and carried around the world in huge tankers. Sometimes there are accidents, and oil gets into the sea and onto beaches. This map shows some of the worst oil spills.

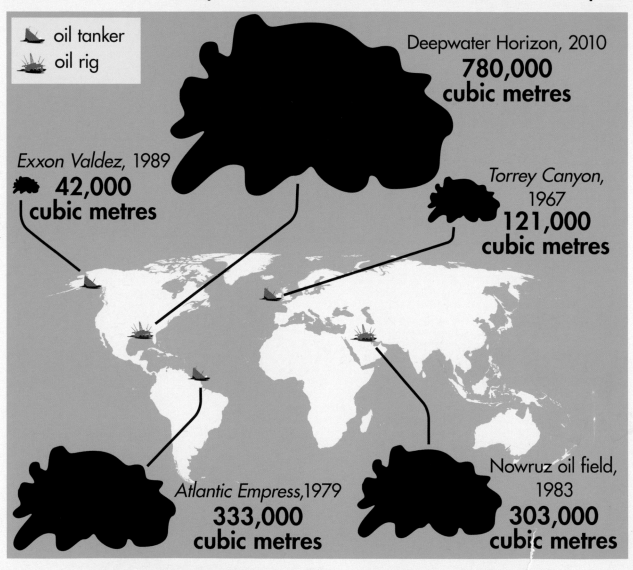

oil tanker
oil rig

Deepwater Horizon, 2010
780,000 cubic metres

Exxon Valdez, 1989
42,000 cubic metres

Torrey Canyon, 1967
121,000 cubic metres

Atlantic Empress, 1979
333,000 cubic metres

Nowruz oil field, 1983
303,000 cubic metres

Noise pollution

Noise isn't the sort of waste you can see or touch. But very loud noise spoils our environment because it is unpleasant and annoying. This infographic shows how loud different noises are.

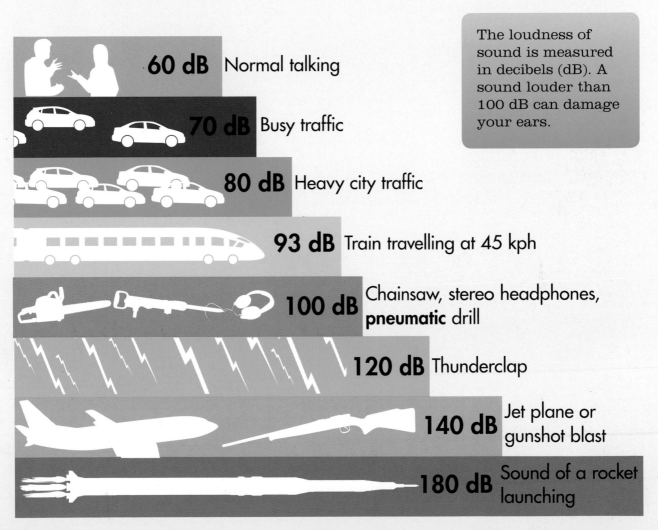

The loudness of sound is measured in decibels (dB). A sound louder than 100 dB can damage your ears.

60 dB Normal talking

70 dB Busy traffic

80 dB Heavy city traffic

93 dB Train travelling at 45 kph

100 dB Chainsaw, stereo headphones, **pneumatic** drill

120 dB Thunderclap

140 dB Jet plane or gunshot blast

180 dB Sound of a rocket launching

ENERGY

We need energy to heat our homes, to make machines and gadgets work, and to travel in cars, trains, and planes. Most of the energy we use comes from oil, coal, and gas. This chart shows the things energy is used for in homes in the United Kingdom.

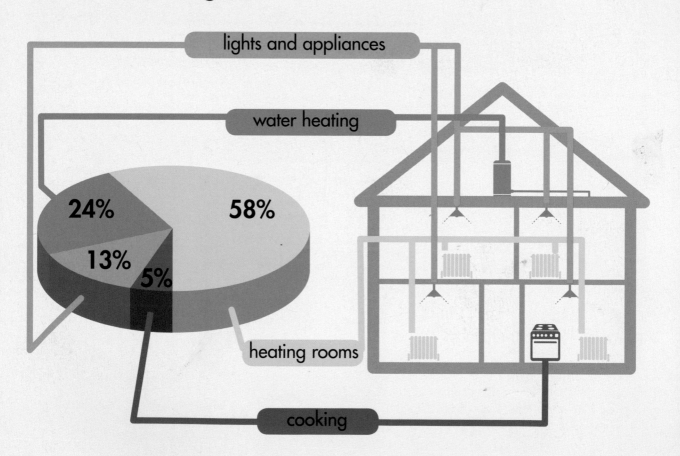

lights and appliances

water heating

24%

58%

13%

5%

heating rooms

cooking

How much electricity we use

This infographic shows how much electricity each person uses every day at home in the United Kingdom.

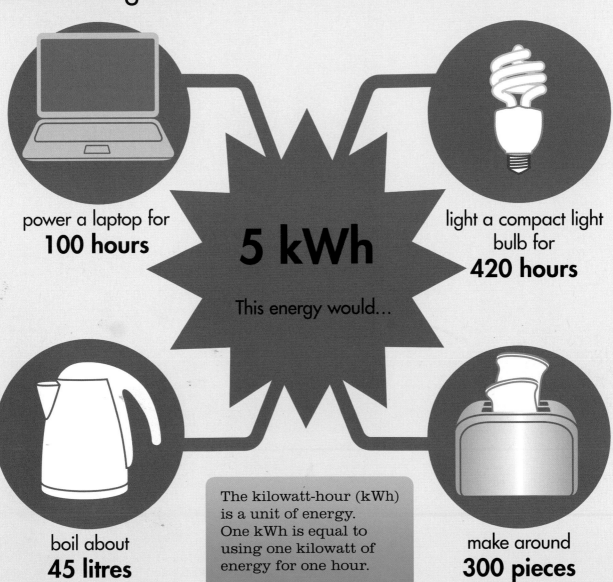

power a laptop for
100 hours

light a compact light bulb for
420 hours

5 kWh

This energy would...

boil about
45 litres
of water in a kettle

make around
300 pieces
of toast

The kilowatt-hour (kWh) is a unit of energy. One kWh is equal to using one kilowatt of energy for one hour.

Where energy comes from

This bar chart shows where the world's energy comes from. Most energy comes from oil, coal, and gas. These are called fossil fuels. Renewable energy includes solar energy and wind energy.

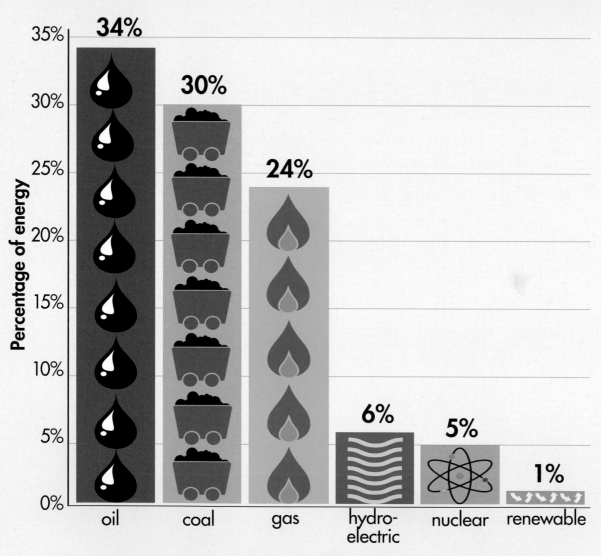

The need for energy

This bar chart shows how the world needs more and more energy each year. It is predicted that energy use will more than double between 1990 and 2035. This is because countries such as China and India are growing fast.

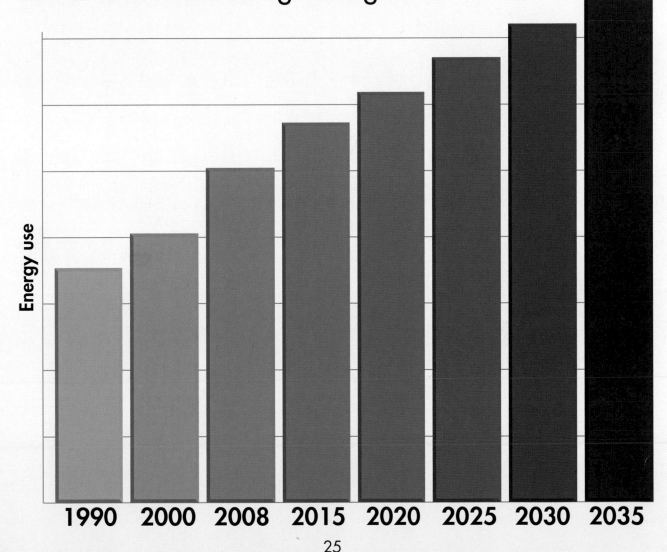

SAVING ENERGY

Using energy is bad for the environment. This is because burning fuels makes **pollution** in the air. If we use less energy, we help the environment. We also spend less money on electricity!

This chart shows different ways of saving energy and how much energy they save.

Only boil as much water as you need. The amount of energy it takes to boil one litre of water could power a fridge for **7 hours**.

Don't leave lights switched on. A 60-watt light bulb left on for one week costs about the same as **2 chocolate bars**.

Cycling 10 kilometres instead of driving saves about **0.7 litres** of fuel.

Insulating the loft of a house could save enough energy each day to make around **400 cups** of tea.

Light bulb energy

This chart shows the amount of energy needed to light different sorts of light bulbs. Bulbs that use less energy are better for the environment.

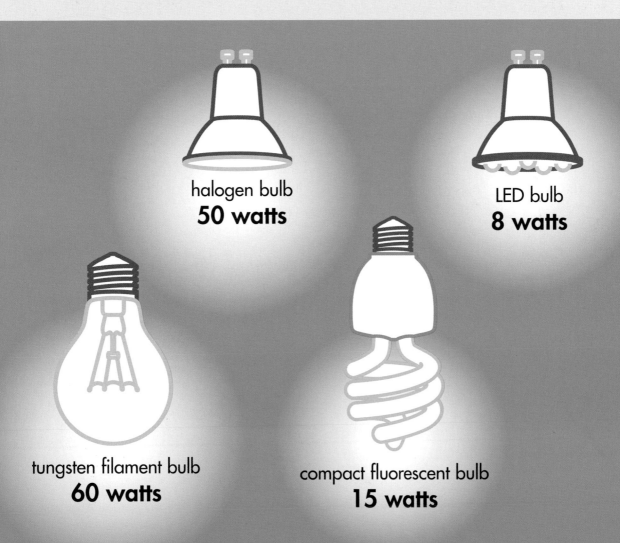

halogen bulb
50 watts

LED bulb
8 watts

tungsten filament bulb
60 watts

compact fluorescent bulb
15 watts

NATURE IN DANGER

Losing the rainforest

The world's rainforests are being chopped down to make space for farming, for mining, and to get wood. This infographic shows how much forest is being chopped down.

130,000 square kilometres of rainforest are lost a year. That is an area the size of England.

That is the same as
36 football pitches per minute

Melting ice

Each year there is less frozen ocean at the North Pole, where animals such as polar bears live. This means polar animals are losing their **habitat**.

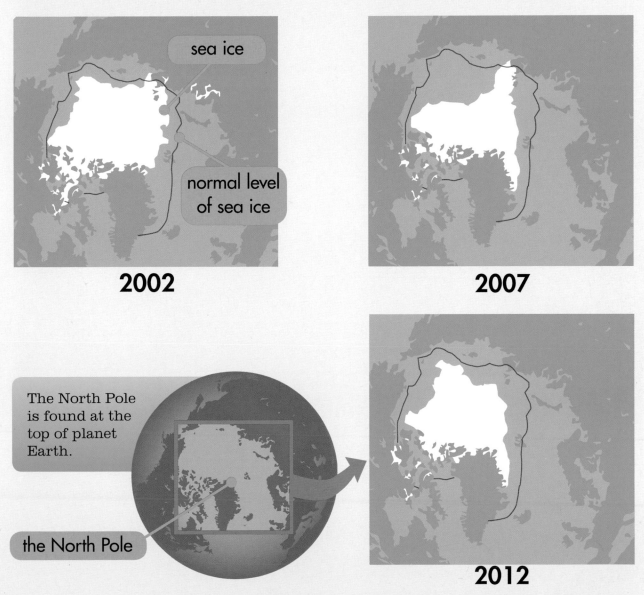

sea ice

normal level of sea ice

2002

2007

The North Pole is found at the top of planet Earth.

the North Pole

2012

GLOSSARY

estimate make a guess about the amount, size, or value of something

habitat place where a plant or animal lives

inorganic not made from plants or animals

landfill waste that is buried in the ground

organic made from plants or animals

pneumatic powered using air

pollution materials that damage the environment, such as plastic and gases from cars

recycle use the materials in an object to make new objects

styrofoam type of plastic used to make cups, food trays and packaging

textile cloth or fabric

trillion number that is equal to one thousand times one billion; 1,000,000,000,000

FIND OUT MORE

Books

Making Graphs (series), Vijaya Khisty Bodach (Capstone Press, 2008)

Rubbish and Recycling (How Does My Home Work?), Chris Oxlade (Raintree, 2013)

Saving Water (Environment Detective Investigates), Jen Green (Wayland, 2010)

Websites

www.recyclezone.org.uk
Find out all about recycling on this website from the Waste Watch organisation.

nces.ed.gov/nceskids/createagraph/default.aspx
Visit this website to create your own graphs and charts.

INDEX